Letters to the Girl in the Mirror

Jaala'Nnette Crenshaw

For the little girl who looked in

the mirror and smiled

before someone told her not to.

Contents

A Brief Introduction

This book is a collection of poems that I've written between the ages of twelve and twenty. Though seemingly a small gap, the number of things I've experienced, felt, and thought within those eight years is comparatively larger. Looking back now, I feel like I was thrown into "adulthood" rather than making an active choice to enter it. Some of these poems express just that while others document specific experiences, desires, or thoughts I've had on my journey from adolescence into adulthood. This book is the record of a frustrated girl who's learning how to navigate a broken world.

There isn't a particular way I've ordered the poems. It's meant to be a bit of a rollercoaster to reflect the quickly changing highs and lows of life. Enjoy the ride.

THIS ISN'T HOW I THOUGHT IT WOULD BE

I was told I could be anything
When I was little.
Five years old with the world at my fingertips–
How come no one told me that this world is so brittle?
As time befriends me, reality becomes me–
But reality isn't as subtle.
He crucifies that world, slowly draining its life: and my mind
He begins to muddle.
I didn't think it would be this hard. It must be me
Because I don't see my brothers struggle.
And my sisters aren't saying anything, they just smile.
I guess I can do that too, and my pain a smile will smuggle.
So I'm touched and admired;
My body is a painting.
You've removed my humanity, my feelings,
I am no more.
That girl dreaming of the change she'd be making
Is gone. And what's left is the shell of person
With no dignity–
But one thought that can change her life if she acts quickly:
This isn't how I thought it would be.

WHITE PICKET FENCE

I love playing in my yard
The grass is so green the air is so sweet
There's so much space, it's so safe
But I always have to stay within the white picket fence

My mom and dad don't usually play with me
They like to watch me from the window
They always remind me how wonderful our yard is
And to always stay within the white picket fence

One day I was playing and I heard a noise
I asked mom and dad about it but they said it was nothing
They told me I was safe in the yard
So I went back to playing behind the white picket fence

The next day I was playing and I heard the noise again
It was really loud this time, a scream
I went to mom and dad and they told me we need to talk
About what was outside the white picket fence

They told me horrible stories
About how they used to have another yard
But they didn't like the rules there
So they gallantly moved to this yard and built a white picket fence

I asked them why they picked this yard
And they told me it was filled with lots of important stuff
And that there were some funny people who gave it all to them
And peacefully left smiling, outside the white picket fence

I asked where they went
They ignored me and told me that anything outside the fence is barbaric
Except some of their friends
But they have their own white picket fence

So I went back outside to play
Proud to be someone who lived inside the fence
I couldn't imagine the horrors
That existed outside the white picket fence

I was playing like usual
When I heard another sound
But this time it wasn't a scream
There was a person standing outside the white picket fence

I was scared to talk to her
After everything mom and dad told me
About the savage creatures
That exist outside the white picket

The girl called again
She didn't sound barbaric
But mom and dad told me
People are good liars outside the white picket fence

But curiosity got the best of me
So when mom and dad weren't looking
I went to talk to the girl
Calling from across the white picket fence

She said her name was Truth
And that she had been sent by her friends
To talk to me about everything that was happening
Outside the white picket fence

I couldn't believe it at first.
She told me that mom and dad were killing people,
And that they stole the yard we live in
Before they built the white picket fence.

I wanted to run inside
And pretend I never heard any of it.
But Truth seemed so plain and bold
So I opened the gate of the white picket fence.

When she followed me in the yard,
Everything started to change.
All the pretty things turned ugly,
And for the first time I wanted to leave the white picket fence.

But Truth told me that for now I needed to stay
And tell everyone about her,
And confront mom and dad about the lies and evil
They had caused everyone outside the white picket fence.

So I told everyone I could find.
But sometimes people laughed
And told me that mom and dad can do whatever they want,
Because everyone was better inside the white picket fence.

But sometimes I found people who listened,
And they listened eagerly!
They asked me how they can help.
I told them to spread the truth about the white picket fence.

Mom and dad became angry
And kept telling lies to anyone that listened.
They said that they were helping not harming
Everyone outside the white picket fence.

But me and my friends didn't believe them anymore.
We protested and shouted about the people dying,
And how mom and dad– Fear and Hatred were the reason
For the oppression that exists outside the white picket fence.

Fear and Hatred tried to stop us,
And sometimes they'd even use force.
But nothing could silence us,
After Truth was brought into the white picket fence.

After some thinking we came up with a plan.
We decided to tear down the white picket fence.
We grabbed whatever we could find,
And started chipping away at the white picket fence.

Some tried to stop us and others joined in.
Two friends– Justice and Knowledge came to help,
And after years of lies,
We finally knocked down the white picket fence.

We were happy to see it gone
But when we looked around us
We still saw pain and suffering
And when we turned, we only saw others' white picket fences.

So now we spend our time shouting
About the lies and atrocities from Fear and Hatred.
But no matter what, me and Truth and Justice and Knowledge won't stop
Until we've broken down every single white picket fence.

HOME

What is home?
I've found myself pondering this question
Recently, do I have one?
Do I need one?
Is it a person, is it a thing, is it a place, what does it mean?
"Where is home for you?"
I find myself at a loss when I'm asked this question.
I think, for a second,
I think, of all the places I've been,
I think, of all the people I've loved,
I think, of all the things I've done,
And still, I cannot think, of an answer to this simple question:
What is home?
I used to think it was a place.
My house, a cluster of rooms filled with the faces I know and love.
I used to think it was a safe space, where I could retire to my room after a
long day,
Or get a snack from the refrigerator after I would play,
Or sit and eat dinner with my family where every night we would pray,
Where I would come home from school, pulling into the driveway,
Where I got ready for my first dance, where I had my worst fight,
Where I laid awake in my bed listening to traumatic whispers through the
night.
So then these dark memories weave their way into the bright
And I ask myself again
What is home?
Maybe it's a person.
Maybe, my home, is my people, my blood.
Maybe it's the people who have laughed with me in my highs and cried with
me in lows.
Maybe it's the people who make sure I know I'm never alone.
Maybe it's my mother who can comfort me with just a hug,
Or maybe it's my father who would tuck me in and scare away the bed bugs.
Or maybe it's my brother who's been on this journey with me from day one,
Or maybe it's my sisters who made every boring day fun.

Maybe my home is the people who brought me into this world and are there
to live through it with me.
Maybe my home is the people who I know I am one of the same,
But these people have brought me pain,
These people have left a stain,
So then these dark memories weave their way into my brain
And I ask myself again
What is home?
I don't know anymore.
The dictionary defines it as "the place where one lives permanently" but my
life impermanent
Am I without a home? Am I without hope?
What is home?
Now I'm all alone, Now I have no place to call my own
Now I am grown
So how could I not have a home?
My home was my house, but then I moved
My home was my family, but I find myself loosed.
I've been displaced from any thought of home,
But I refuse to accept this thought.
I refuse the idea that I could be without an origin, to be without a cause,
without a meaning.
So I ask myself once more:
What is home?
I find my answer to this question continually changing yet I have never *felt*
homeless. I have never *felt* alone. I have always had people that I call my
own.
My home is always changing but my home is always the same.
My home has always been filled with joy even when there was pain.
Perhaps my home is chaotic and messy in all its glory
But I am sure that I have a home,
I know because I have a story.
And every story has a cause,
Every story has a purpose,
Every story has a beginning and end.
And I know that even through my story as I roam,
I am never lost because I have a home.

NIGHT

Give me the moon, you can have the sun.
If I could have the stars, the light I would shun.

Give me the cool, give me dark.
Take the blue skies, I'll take the stark.

You can have the warm upon your skin,
But I want the mystery of the howling wind.

Give me a path lit by fair moonlight,
Give it to me, and you take my sight.

Take all the animals loved and adored,
And give me the Nocturnals the light ignores.

You take the comfort, I'll take the fear,
When your people hide, I'll wipe their tears.

You can have reality, I want the dreams
That drown out your world with a sweet moonbeam.

You take the goodness, and I'll take the wicked.
I'll have the shameful acts committed.

For my world is truth and your world is fake.
Which world is better? the line is opaque.

But I choose the dark, you can have the light.
You prefer the day, but I love the night.

In Love

I used to say that I can't wait until I fall in love
So I can write the type of poetry I love to read.
But recently I've realized that there's a reason I so dearly love words of
devotion and affection.
It's because I've already experienced it–
In the form of the women I so blessedly call *friend*.

The ones who taught me that love is free,
The ones who laugh and suffer with me,
The ones who hold me late at night,
When watching a movie, hugging me tight.
The ones who don't bat an eye when I'm acting insane.
The ones whose relationships aren't an ounce of a strain.
The ones who help me love myself as they do.
The ones who hold my heart gracefully no matter what we go through.

Yes, there's a beauty to the lust and passion of romance,
But my friends have already taught me what it means to be in love.
Maybe one day I'll find someone for whom I'll walk down the aisle,
But I already know the faces of the women that I'll look up through my veil
and see, smiling at me.

Lost

I am lost
Wandering through this endless maze
Turning without reason
Aimless and mundane
I'm looking for a purpose
Am I looking for a person?
Either way I am unsuccessful
And with each turn my panic worsens
When I started this maze
I thought it would be effortless
My path was straight
But it quickly turned into this current mess
Am I all alone?
Is there any escape?
I can't take this pointless nothingness
Any longer, this void with no shape
I take one final turn
And I'm ready to give in
There is only darkness ahead of me
Then I hear a voice from within:

Nothing is pointless.
Your life has purpose.
Continue on your path.
You are so much more than worthless.

So I take another step.
I still have no drive.
Then I take another turn.
A small light, I'll survive.

AUTUMN

I was once young and naive,
I was silly to believe what I believed.

I dreamt of a life of endless youth,
Where the sun was always shining, but that was never my truth.

I was always destined to be what I am now.
Oh, how I wish I could go back to being foolish and proud.

But I'm no longer what I used to be.
I'm old and burnt out, barely hanging from my tree.

My bright color is gone, and my old life is too.
I'm just waiting to fall, to make room for the new.

I know that I'm admired but I don't want to go.
They call me beautiful, but I don't think so.

Sure, my color brings thoughts of sweaters and coffee,
And my friends are all ready, but no, not me.

So I hold on for as long as I can.
I breathe in the laughter for the rest of my span.

But I can't hold on forever, it's getting harder to stay.
Then slowly I feel myself slipping away…

I feel myself falling but it wasn't what I thought,
It's peaceful so I ponder the new life that I once fought.

And soon enough I'm on the ground.
I don't feel that special with all my peers around.

But then a child comes my way,
He jumps on me, and laughs something beautiful, and my fear melts away.

I'm no longer young and vibrant or even alive,
But the joy that I invoke brushes all that aside.

This new life called death has always been my fate:
To bring the autumn that the people await.

FEELING

I wake up and I'm sad.
You ask me how I am and I'm happy sad.
For just a moment I'm happy happy.
But reality sinks in
And I'm happy sad sad.
I carry on and I'm happy happy sad.
I'll smile at you like I'm happy happy happy sad.
Then someone asks and it slips
I'm sad sad.
I'm sad scared guilty.
So next time I'm happy happy happy happy happy sad.
But it's so hard when I'm tired tired sad.
So I'm drained.
And I'm nothing.
Cause I can't keep feeling happy happy sad happy sad.
So I stop feeling.
Well what's better:
Feeling, faking, or nothing?
Why can't I just be free?
Why can't I be happy happy?
I tried but I became happy tired sad.
Maybe I'm just not supposed to be happy happy.
Maybe I'll always be sad sad.
But I hope one day I'll be free free free.
And I'll feel feel feel.
So I guess I'm happy sad hopeful.
I'll be free when I can feel sad happy scared guilty tired drained nothing
brave.
Because for me, freedom is fearless feeling.

THE AXE

I think I would rather someone hate me than not care about me at all.
After all, isn't apathy the opposite of love?

I would rather have my name screamed than never spoken at all,
Cause at least then I'd be known.

I would rather you look into my eyes with resentment than not look into my
eyes at all.
Cause at least then you'd see me.

The pain from indifference always hurt so much more than the pain from
abhorrence.
Because at least I could make it up to you when you finally thought of me.

Well that's how I would imagine it– if it ever happened.
But I'm a broken tree in a forest with no witness.

GRAY SKIES

I'm happy and I smile and I laugh– my life is great.
I breathe in, taste the crisp air, just another perfect day.
But what's that gray spot in the sky, towering high?
It's far away, I think it's safe to say
It's nothing.
Everything's just fine.

I'm ambitious, I dream big, and I work hard for what I want.
I take pride in my aspirations, in each and every accomplishment.
What was that? "What?" I think I saw it move. You disapprove?
You're right, it's nothing. It's nothing?
It's nothing.
Everything's just fine.

I'm loved, by my family, my friends. They care.
So why can't they see that cloud over there?
They only see blue skies, the sunrise.
          I'm traumatized.
I'll push it aside. They don't realize. I'll compromise.
It's nothing
Everything's just fine.

"What's wrong? Smile. Enjoy the moment while you can."
You're right. Why am I sad? What's wrong with me? Life is grand.
Why won't this cloud go away? Please, just for today? Don't stay here.
I'm happy. Look at me smile. Hear me laugh. They all fall for my perfect
scam.
It's nothing. Go away.
Everything's just fine.

It's storming. I can't ignore it anymore, like I did before.
No more smile, no more laugh. There's nothing left. I'm done for.
This stupid cloud, is screaming aloud. I am lost.
What do I do? Who do I tell? I don't want to burden them. I don't want to ask
for
Help!
Nothing is fine.

"You look like you've been struggling with things. Let me in. I'm just here to listen.
I'm here to be here. I'm not going anywhere. Let me in."
I'm desperate so I begin:
You see, I have this cloud that won't go away. And it burdens me. And keeps me captive.
"I see it." You see it? The rain stops. The cloud's still there but the sun peaks through.
It's not nothing,
But things will be just fine.

You see I have a gray cloud too. We all do, but it looks yours grew.
You just can't help it no matter what you do, but I see your storm and I'll share it with you.
What's that? A clear sky? I haven't seen one in quite some time.
My storm is gone, and the sun's peaked through, I can see the sky, I see its blue hue.
This world is something.
Even with clouds it's truly divine.

SAVANNAH

"Savannah, I'm going Home."
How strange those words feel
Forming in my mouth,
Because Savannah was once
Albany, and Albany was once
Birmingham, and Birmingham was once
St. Louis, and I don't remember before that.

Savannah, Albany, Birmingham, St. Louis:
How naturally the list rolls off of my tongue.
How used to change–impermanence I am.
How unorthodox it feels to stand still.

Savannah– how sweet it sounds now,
When a year ago it was just another city
I couldn't list.
Savannah– how strange it is flying
From one home
To another,
From a home that I've established
To a Home that was established twenty-three
Years ago
By my parents.
And then back I'll go to the home
That I'm still making my own.

Savannah, I've never even lived there.
They left me behind.
Or was it me?

Savannah, the small little airport
Right near the border
Of the state where my family lives–
One-thousand miles away from my home in Boston,
Only one-hundred-sixty-nine miles from Albany,
Where I couldn't wait to leave,
And now I can't wait to go home.

Savannah, I'm going Home.

KINTSUGI

How treacherously my heart turns from one master to another.
From Savior to Sin, Maker to Malignity.
How brokenly my soul looks away,
Mangledly running back to its Father,
       Fighting the demons of self-hatred,
       Fighting for hope of grace.

How naturally my heart takes on the burdens of the world.
Opening its expansive chasms to whomever may need a home,
Content to eternally pour itself out,
Regardless of the nothingness it receives in return.
       Teary eyed,
       Chipping itself away with a smile.

How can these two strings pull me so insistently?
The two forces battle and I don't know who I am.
A puppet for love?
Or a puppet for wickedness?
       I can't rid myself of either.
       Am I eternally doomed to this duality?

How can this burden be taken from me so graciously?
Come and see this broken vessel pour once again!
A desperately wicked heart and a love like my Maker's,
Brushed aside as my Savior pours out that I may too.
       Come and see
       This broken vessel pour once again!

I'M YOURS

Sometimes people say "I am yours" without a thought,

But when I say "I am yours" I mean that if you lived in some ancient city, I'd
be the forest around you, so you could use my wood to warm your home, to
make the spoon with which you eat, to build your ships to see the world, to
burn on the altar of your sacrifices.

If you were a knight in some high castle, I'd be the mines that your people
cut through for the metal used in your armor and weapons that protect you,
the cup from which you drink, the mirror in which you look, the crown
placed on your head.

If you somehow became wicked, I'd be the shadow that follows you in the
day and sings your praise into the winds of the night, that hides your sins
from the world, that caresses your face to show its beauty, that keeps you
from being burned.

I'd be content as the wood in your hands, about to be burned so long as you
hold me–
The metal on your head, carved from its home, so long as I know your mind–
The shadow that follows you, that people run from, so long as I am your
home.

ON GROWING OLD

I used to be afraid of growing old
When I was a little girl.
Cause if I wasn't beautiful
I would have no value in this world.

At least that's the picture I saw.
The puzzle pieces awkwardly fit–
No, awkwardly *forced*, to create a likeness
That I'm still trying to unknit.

But today I was riding the train
And an old woman smiled at me.
I beheld her, looking so picturesque
And so incredibly happy.

She was nothing to fear,
Rather something to behold.
I tug on a piece of the jigsaw
Breaking out of the mold.

MOTHERLY ADORATION

No one at all prepares you for the day
When the role between mother and daughter
Is reversed.

One day I'm five years old–
I stumble in front of my mother–
"Do you like my dress, mom?"
She doesn't even look up–
Rather than engaging her eyes on her daughter,
She rolls them.
"You're so vain."
I blink– a tear– I'm twenty.

"Look at my new overalls"
The notification comes through my phone–
I open the text to see my mother smiling–
Posing in mossy green overalls.
She's beautiful. And I tell her.
It's not hard to love her.
I turn off my phone– I'm five again.

She hadn't even looked at me.
I lock myself in the bathroom so she can't hear me crying.
My heart is heavy with want and hurt disguised as anger.
I gaze into the mirror. Why wouldn't she look at me?
Why wouldn't she look into the eyes that were her own.
Did she hate herself? Or did she hate me?

I open my phone again–
I look into her eyes–
The brown half of mine–
With a motherly adoration–
I tell her how beautiful they are–
Like I practiced in the mirror so many times–

MOVEMENT

I don't think I would trade my emotional depth for anything.
I feel everything so potently.
Joy-
Anger-
Peace-
Pain-
All of it.
When I'm happy my heart could replace the sun,
And brighten an entire galaxy.
And when I hurt the weight of my heart could break the laws of gravity
And sink the entire universe.

But most importantly–
I can see everything–
Written on the faces–
On the folds of every movement–
Of anyone I encounter–
I can see the sculpts cut into a person where they hurt the most–
I can see the light shining through the parts that are purely love–
All of it.
And the way a person is moved when I look into their eyes and know them–
And *feel* them–
I wouldn't trade it for anything.

WINDOWS AND CURTAINS

They say that your eyes are a window into the soul.
But they never talk about how we all use curtains.

We can just smile and we're fully in control.
Of what we see in someone's eyes we can never be certain.

IMPOSSIBLE CHANGE

When child becomes grown,
  And later forgets all they've known,
When sunlight turns to snow,
  And the winds of change begin to blow,
When man and woman love,
  And two becomes one,
When day turns to night,
  And likewise, blindness to sight,
When life turns to death,
  And we give up our breath–
Why is that we are always becoming that which we never were–
That which we never could have been–
That which faces us in the contrary mirror–
  Suddenly I don't recognize the person whose gaze has mine
  clutched in her talons–
  Her prey because I forgot to–
  But I know her.
  She hates me, but I'm all she's ever wanted to be.
As contrary becomes same–
As never becomes now.

PROJECTOR

For some reason I can't remember.
Memories fade like dying embers.

Whether from trauma and pain
Or just the disconnect in my brain,

I can't hold on to the things I've done.
So I question the life my mind has spun.

Is any of it even real?
I can't trust the things I feel.

So then where did the feelings come from?
If none of it happened wouldn't I be numb?

What if I trusted the feelings that always remain,
And follow the trail they've so passionately lain.

When I lean into one, it's like an explosion,
A haunting cavern of ceaseless emotion.

And suddenly I'm transported to ages past.
My mind becomes a projector for the memories it can finally cast.

FOR YOU I WOULD

"For you I would–"
Said Paolo to Francesca, bracing himself to spend an eternity in Hell,
Hand in hand, pages on the floor.

"For you I would–"
Said Adam to Eve, not bothering to gaze upon the garden again,
Hand in hand, apple bitten.

"For you I would–"
Said Mark to Cleopatra, throwing down his shield to give up his nation forever,
Hand in hand, war waged.

"For you I would–"
Said Richard to Mildred, bags packed and ready to leave everything behind,
Hand in hand, court in session.

"For you I would–"
I say to you, opening my heart when I thought I never could, to give you anything,
Hand in hand, broken restored.

"…Wherever the wind may take us."

CLOUDY SKIES

Why do you look so sad?
What makes you mourn so?
When I see you, the feelings I had
Dissipate and I have to let them go.

Why are you weeping?
For are you not filled?
When you cry my heart starts leaping
And everything around me is stilled.

Why are you gray,
And why are you blue,
When you lead the way
For the life you renew?

Bringer of life
And of romance,
You remove all strife
And replace it with dance.

How could anyone hate you?
I love you dearly.
They simply don't know
That you are so much more than dreary.

I know you are broken,
But my joy stems from your pain.
Your droplets tell stories unspoken
Pour down your sweet rain.

LOSING MYSELF

I can't count the number of times I've been asked
What advice I'd give my younger self.
But she's already passed, she's already been failed.
What about me now?
What advice do I give the girl
Who's trying to navigate this world
While healing past ones?

I find myself listening in
When others give their aged advice,
Trying to find bits and pieces I can swallow
And digest into my mind's eye
So that it might open and see some golden way,
Or a yellow brick road–
Fuck, I'd even settle for some beaten dirt path–
Breadcrumbs even–
Just something–
Anything–

I just need something that keeps me
Here–
That keeps me together–
Cause every time I look down I see
My hand pulsing with my heart–
Expanding and contracting as hard as it can to run away–
Like an eager little caterpillar ready to be a butterfly–
But I don't have a chrysalis–
I'm not ready for any kind of metamorphosis–
Cause every time I look up
I see my hair blowing in the wind,
Wisping off the few neurons I have left–
Strands statically sending off cells–
Axons to dendrites–
And there I go losing my mind.

My heart and my mind are turning on me
Just as I thought I understood them–
And my body is overseeing the coup
Just as I started to love her.

I'm losing myself.
Just as I started to get that little girl back.
I need my older self to come visit me now because
I'm losing myself.
And my body, heart, and mind have run away
So it's too late to share them with anyone–
I'm losing myself.

I think all I have left is my soul .
But I'm still trying to understand that.
No matter how many philosophers I read or poets I feel,
My soul is so much more than thoughts or feelings.
But I'm trying to know her and trying to love her,
Cause she's so known and so loved.
My soul is grounding me.

I'm trying to find myself.

BECOMING

Every moment of my life I've waited for the next.
Growing into tomorrow's version of myself.
My every being, never *being*.
But *becoming*.

SWEET DREAMS

I had a dream that I was in a forest,
Branches far surpassing my head,
With canopies of green and beams of gold,
And my dress was made of dandelion thread.

I had a dream that I sprouted wings,
Big and strong yet light and fluorescent,
As the nerves attached they began to move,
Each flap like the moon increscent.

I had a dream that my feet left the ground,
No weight I carried anymore.
It was all blown into the wind
Or left with my shadow on the forest floor.

I had a dream that I journeyed high,
The world grew small and my perspective shifted,
Nothing seemed quite so urgent anymore,
Now that I and my soul had been lifted.

I had a dream that I brushed the trees,
Their tops became a leafy field,
So I flew and frolicked under the sun,
Once a mystery now unconcealed.

I had a dream I saw something down below,
Rich red with spots of white,
It seemed to call me from beneath the trees,
So I began to descend my flight.

I had a dream that I touched the ground,
I looked up and couldn't believe my eyes,
Before me stood a little mushroom house,
With lanterns lit by dragonflies.

I had a dream I opened the door,
And oh what splendor I beheld,
The perfect cottage for a girl like me,
I giggled with excitement as my heart swelled.

I had a dream that I wanted a treat,
So off to the kitchen I scurried,
With acorn bowls and tiny twig mixers,
Dusting and folding, my fingers hurried.

I had a dream that the oven dinged,
And out popped my little scone,
Filled with berries and icing on top,
It melted in my mouth with flavors I had never known.

I had a dream that I heard a knock,
So I opened the little mushroom door,
And there stood a round beetle in a suit,
And an emerald tie around his core.

I had a dream I welcomed him inside,
Around a cherry birch bark table,
On walnut stools we sat,
And ate as many scones as we were able.

I had a dream that my eyes weighed heavy,
And out came a little yawn,
Off went Mr. Beetle into the night,
I jumped in my cozy moss bed and dreamed until the dawn.

SHADOWS

Why is it that we so dearly love the light?
Is it because it protects us from shadows,
Or because it creates them?

A forest isn't habitable until its branches writhe up and out
To take the beating of the light and heat,
Conceiving a canopy of damp darkness so the earth below can take its first
breaths,
Cold and merciful.

A siren doesn't become a legend with just a smile–
No, it's not until her dripping lips roll like waves across her face to reveal a
cave of jagged teeth, fresh with the flesh of her newest victim,
Bloody and refined.

A raven will always be more beloved than a dove,
Because purity could never be more than a competition, for who can be most
complicit in the infringement of unorthodox norms.
Blind and sedated.

Is there not an ugliness hidden in blinding light and a beauty that is passed by
in the winding night? But are they not most bewitching when intertwined–
Like magic.
The forest, siren, and raven, loved and feared, shadowed and weird.

MIRROR

When you are left crying alone
Who wipes your tears?
When you have been abandoned
Who calms your fears?
When your trust has been broken,
When you wish promises were left unspoken,
When the world against you has turned
Who do you look to?
When you have been forgotten and burned
Who stays with you?
So tell my why when you look in the mirror
you hate what you see
When the answer to each question is "me"?

OXYGEN

Before I knew what air was,
I breathed.
Every day of my life, completely unaware,
I have breathed.
Without hesitation, without pause,
I breathe.
I am surrounded by air,
So I breathe.

The air was always there for me,
So I always just presumed,
Perpetually filling my lungs,
With every molecule I consumed.

So I wasn't at all prepared,
For the day that it wasn't there,
The day my lungs were bare,
Devoid of any air.

I suffocated,
Violently thrashing,
Without any air,
My world was crashing.

And crash it did.
I was never the same.
That day the air wasn't there,
He took the blame.

But that day did not kill me.
Air did return.
But I was changed,
And left with a burn.

A burn that took away hope.
A burn that took away trust.
A burn that made me question.
A burn that left me crushed.

But even the broken keep breathing.
There is healing for the deepest burn.
So no matter how hard I try to breathe without it,
To the air I always return.

I'm still perplexed by Air,
But I breathe.
Every day of my life, though I am scared,
I breathe.
Filled with hesitation, always wanting to pause,
I must breathe.
I am surrounded by both pain and air,
So I breathe.

UNCHANGEABLE

I hope that your heart breaks like mine does. I hope that you shiver from the cold air of the depths to which I've been driven. I hope that your tongue is frozen and your eyes become melting glaciers, just as mine have. I hope that you are moved as I am moved. I hope that you feel what I feel. I hope that you weep with me. But I know that you will not change as I am changed. So that you can take it when I cannot.

Palabras

"Con…tigo,"
Las palabras estaban frescas
De sus labios.
No pensó en ellas,
No tenían peso.
"¿Conmigo qué?" Silencio.
Entonces "todo," entonces nada.

"With… you,"
The words were fresh
From your lips.
You didn't think about them,
They had no weight.
"With me what?" Silence.
Then "everything," then nothing.

ICARUS

I'd fall forever to feel his warmth.
I'd die again for just a touch.
I'd drown once more for just a kiss.
I'd burn for eternity to have him in my clutch.

I fell in love with who he was.
Everyone else saw him for his light and glory.
But he was so much more than just the sun.
I know that he loved and adored me.

I was young when I fell in love,
I didn't know what I was doing.
He was so perfect, he understood it all,
But I didn't know what I'd be losing.

It was never going to work,
Our love was always doomed,
But he chose me over all the rest.
Maybe it would've been easier if he loved the moon.

But he chose me for reasons I'll never know.
And even though I lost it all,
I'd choose this love in any life.
Until eternity ends I'll throw myself into his thrall.

His destiny was set in stone.
Mine was still in the making.
But our love was so strong, I didn't care,
If it was my life he'd be taking.

I flew for him,
And he burned for me,
And though it was just a moment,
The story of our love will last for eternity.

I felt his flame, I knew his embrace
And the moment we touched I fell from above.
But my fate was sealed, and I was satisfied,
As long as he knew what it was like to be loved.

And though I am gone,
My love for him still burns.
But we both once loved each other,
And for each other we'll forever yearn.

BUT THE GREATEST OF THESE IS LOVE

I chose love.
It was like scaling the highest mountain on Jupiter.
I choose love.
It's like Hades waiting for Persephone every Spring.
I will always choose love.
It'll be like the fulfillment of the wisping embrace of Paolo and Francesca.
I will prevail every single time.
Because of love.

فماذا عندنا؟

ليس هناك كتاب عن كيف نعيش الحياة

ليس هناك أغنية عن كيف نتكلم

ليس هناك قصة عن كيف نحب

فماذا عندنا؟ سوى تجاربنا لنتعلم

للأسوأ أم للأفضل

There is no book on how we live life

There is no song on how we speak

There is no story on how we love

So what do we have? But our experiences to teach us

For better or for worse

FRIEND'S FLAME

I walked through this hopeless earth
In almost complete darkness
Lit only by my own flame
Met by dwindling starkness.

My light burned as bright as it could
From a flame that so many times,
Had been so carelessly blown out
By others' hatred-filled crimes.

But still my flame continued to burn bright
Holding on to every drop of fuel,
Trying as hard to ignite others as it could
Without receiving anything back, like a naive fool.

Soon my foolish flame realized
That no flame made it burn like it did them,
And was dwindled by the lack of love
Believing it was to eternal neglect condemned.

Until one fatefully sealed day
Almost burned out completely,
I saw a flame shining bright in the distance,
Burning so purely and sweetly.

I ran desperately to meet this flame,
Naivety and desperation begging to try
To love and light someone once more,
Any acknowledgement of pain defied.

I plunged my crushed flame
Deeply into hers,
Holding my breath,
Waiting for nothing in return.

But immediately I felt something inside of me
Burning bright and intense.
My flame burned brighter than it ever had
Filled with a love that doesn't make sense.

There was something divine within her,
Because I felt a light like never before.
I've found a flame in a friend,
She's all I could ever dream of and more.

A Day in My Head's Dizziness

Making my mental checklist
Checking for what I might have missed
Miss Lynne texted me last week and I never answered
Answer that email by the end of the day
Day, Day, Day, Day,
Sunday, Monday, Tuesday, Wednesday, Thursday, *Friday*, Saturday
"What did you say? Huh?"
They're mad,
Why are they standing like that
They just looked at your shirt
They probably think you're fat
Remember the Cat in the Hat?
I used to love that show
Show me a *sign*
Hit me baby one more time
I'm hungry
Time to eat
What do I want?
Make a plan,
Heat up the pan,
Pan on the stove,
Cut the garlic clove,
We're almost out of milk
Milk, granola, eggs apparently,
Apparently I've never been on live television,
And it was *great*
Great, I just spilled juice on my white shirt,
Shit, where did that bruise come from?
I wonder if mom is mad at me.
Probably.
What do I need to do?
Do the dishes,
Clean my room?
Party on Friday,
Shopping on Saturday
Church on Sunday
Work on Monday
REMEMBER THE TIME YOU FELL DOWN THE STAIRS
Can you shut the fuck up?
Up, up, up, up, up, up, up

Thump, thump, thump, thump, thump…
Mom, mom, mom, mom,
I can't breathe, what's happening,
Mom, answer please…
One, two, three, four, five, six, seven…
One two three…
Inhale, hold, exhale, hold
One, two three, four five,
Breathe, breathe, breathe, breathe, breath.
One
Two
Three
Four
Five
Six
Seven
Eight
Nine
Ten
Heartbreak is one thing, my ego's another…
So I fall in love just a little oh, little bit every day with someone new…
One, two, three, four, five, six, seven…
"Hmm?"
"Oh, nothing."

Healing

Every bite.
Every smile in the mirror.
Every promiscuous top.
Every "I forgive you."
Every cheek-staining tear.
Every "I love you as you are…"
I put a band-aid over the chasms carved in my heart.
And watch it heal.
Word by word.
Drop by drop.
Day by day.

MOSAIC

My best friend's favorite color is blue.
We talk over meals and art at museums.
My heart is blue.

My Dad's favorite color is purple.
We talk about life and sip our coffees.
My mind is purple.

My Mom's favorite color is orange.
We rearrange the house and play card games.
My hands are orange.

My sister's favorite color is lilac.
We watch movies and do our makeup.
My eyes are lilac.

My favorite color is green.
I spend my life with the people I love.
My body is a mosaic of those who have painted their colors on my canvas.

POMEGRANATE

One–
No more light.
No more lying in a meadow,
As sunbeams gently trace my skin like the rising and falling of ocean waves.
No more golden hour,
When the dark brown spots in my eyes, melt into honey, and the deep green,
blooms into flakes of fern.
No more galleries,
At dawn or dusk, where colors unimaginable, are painted across the
impermanent, sinking blue canvas, each stroke like a grain of sand falling
from the hourglass, staining the beauty of change.

Two-
No more innocence.
No more following behind my mother,
With my hand in hers, learning to love, and loving to learn.
No more childhood,
Without responsibility, following my heart wherever it may take me, without
a care– without any notice, of the shadows that creep on my blazing
footsteps.
No more chastity,
Wandering without want, unknown to all– a mystery, hair unbound, wildly
winding down my back, just as I came– the state in which I entered the
world, my own.

Three-
No more life.
No more flora and fauna,
Maturing by the work of my own hand, watered by the sweat of my brow.
No more progress,
Gazing ambitiously into the future, working for the next achievement, like
markings on the wall, where you once looked up with excitement and now
look down with pride.
No more breath,
Lungs filling with air, lifting you off the ground, and gliding back down as
the air leaves, blowing away the waste that once held you down, your pulse
now, rhythmic and steady.

Four–
Bring on death.
Bring on stillness,
The eternal rest after a lifetime of movement– peace.
Bring on permanence,
Where I never have to count my hours, and I never wonder when the sun will set, because I know I'm safe, nothing can hurt me anymore– trust.
Bring on the inevitable,
The destination where we all end up anyways, regardless of where we were, *who* we were, what we had, all of it, washed away in the river, that steers us here– *telos*.

Five–
Bring on power.
Bring on significance,
Where my words carry importance, because I'm not just another girl anymore.
Bring on the crown,
A kingdom, swarming with souls, to care for, to cherish, to know– chosen, elected, because I'm capable, I'm worthy.
Bring on choice,
Completely, absolutely my own– my hands at my sides, extended only when I wish them to be–
They are the hands that take care of me, no one else's.

Six–
Bring on darkness.
Bring on apathy,
Where I no longer care to look into a mirror, because it's not my beauty that people judge.
Bring on truth,
Where things that shine do so of their own artistry, not lit by charming rays that disappear at dusk.
Bring on intimacy,
Because when it's cold I reach for hands to hold mine, to warm me, to feel me, and they will– I know the hands I reach for, because in the darkness, everything is as it seems, and I have nothing to distract me from what sits just ahead– they'll hold me however long I need them to– until they kill me– a small death.

The Mirror of My Heart

When do we become responsible for self correction?
Is it when we depart from our parent's protection?
Or is it a choice we come to on our own?
When we see ourselves in the mirror, when we're grown?
Before I became destructively self-aware
It was my parents who taught me what was fair.
And whenever I departed from that line
My punishment came from their decisions without a thought of how it might
affect mine.

I was spanked, I was lectured, and sometimes hugged at the end
A few times they told me I was worthy of love no matter how many rules I
bend.
But since I can remember, my reactions to my own sins
Have been hateful extremities responding to the lies my mind spins.
"You deserve to hurt." Pain was to be the decree,
Because somehow I convinced myself that everyone was worthy of love,
except for me.
Somehow my brain has equated failure with harm,
And my heart knows it's crazy but this active intrusion is difficult to unarm.

And here I am now, a wise and clueless twenty years old,
Still trying to unlearn the patterns of self-hatred my heart so wearily holds.
And even though it varies from day to day,
Sometimes I like who I see in the mirror and the hatred starts to decay.
My mind has started to tell me things my heart doesn't believe,
Like words of my beauty and worth despite what others may perceive.
But even though it's not something my heart always accepts
I'll remedy the poison with self-care and self-love because those are the first
steps.

ATLAS

I thought I carried tons in my hands,
But my mother is Atlas.
She was given a world to hold just as she was ready to skip out of the galaxy.
So what if she gave me a paltry piece of the planet–
She continued to carry the world that I lived in–
Laboring until she was Hercules–
But even Hercules is human.
My mother is Atlas.

NAMES

Jaala Belle…
That's what my Maw Maw used to call me
When I was little
Because I was beautiful.
And I was beautiful
Wasn't I?
When I looked in the mirror
I was pure
Because I hadn't learned the word ugly yet.
The world hadn't taught me to hate myself.

Jaala'Nnette!
That's what my mom called me
When she was mad.
I had learned the word ugly.
Jaala'Nnette!
I had *felt* the word ugly.
But wasn't I still beautiful?

Stupid…
My brother would call me when I was
Being annoying,
But it had no weight, he was my brother.

Too much.
My mom called me when I was…
Being myself,
It was the weight of the world, she was my mother.

Too much what?
I asked myself.
I was a girl.
I am a woman.
Too much what?
Was I beautiful?

Jaala'Nnette…
That's what the people who love me call me.

My mom has started to call me
Jaala'Nnette.
I am beautiful.

www.ingramcontent.com/pod-product-compliance
Lightning Source LLC
Chambersburg PA
CBHW051500140726
47987CB00006B/2798